GOODBYE TO THE ART OF POETRY

POETRY BY PETER LEVI

Collected Poems 1955–1975
Five Ages
Private Ground
The Echoing Green
Shakespeare's Birthday
Shadow and Bone

PETER LEVI

Goodbye to the Art
of Poetry

ANVIL PRESS POETRY

Published in 1989
by Anvil Press Poetry Ltd
69 King George Street London SE10 8PX

Set in Bembo by Anvil
Printed and bound in England
by The Arc & Throstle Press, Todmorden

This book is published
with financial assistance from
The Arts Council of Great Britain

British Library Cataloguing in Publication Data

Levi, Peter, 1931 –
  Goodbye to the art of poetry.
  I. Title
  821'.914

ISBN 0 85646 212 8

FOR DEIRDRE

*Goodbye to the Art
of Poetry*

ROBERT GRAVES said there can be no long poem
and that Virgil and Milton who wrote them
were tying short poems together with string.
How long after all does any bird sing?
The machine of a poem is not natural:
the mysterious bird-call, the apple's fall
reach out from earth and the sun towards death,
a perfect poem is a dying breath:
and yet it lives as long as music can,
say three days of the chanting of a blind man,
holding within it an image of time:
the god sleeps and the bell may never chime.
Leningrad, its heart of snow and railways,
one star of violet trembling in that haze,
spreads from one stanza into many days.
Pax Britannica, wild roses, coal:
Milton ebbing and thundering in the soul,
poems longer than a wax light can burn,
poems it takes a human life to learn.
Yet it remains true the genuine sign
of greatness in a poem is one line.
    What poetry and what greatness may be
bothers all professors of poetry:
there is something ridiculous I confess
in sharp-eyed connoisseurship of greatness:

better to seek for what is genuine:
a world spacious enough to wander in,
the truth live in the ear as truth of tone,
a line that rings like stone ringing on stone
or a line like the sea heard in a shell,
never again so clearly or so well
as it was in the beginning, in childhood,
when poetry was the untrodden wood:
Seasons return, but not to me returns
Day, or the sweet approach of Ev'n or Morn,
Or sight of vernal bloom, or Summers Rose,
Or flocks, or herds, or human face divine . . .
Milton, poet of the spirit's expense,
youthful intellect and sharpness of sense,
truth to age, truth to experience,
in whom all learning, rhetoric and belief
have been drowned out in the knowledge of life,
sea-pebbles, sea-coarsened and sea-refined,
long rhythms of a man lonely and blind
whose paradise might not be lingered in:
he felt death in his eyes, dawn on his skin,
cold, wild poetry like the Atlantic,
archangelic construction of music:
intellectual myth, necromancy:
this is greatness and truth in poetry.
Milton's age was like Raleigh's in the Tower,
a man defeated, high on love of power.
In the dark seed of poetry is pride:

remember Mayakovsky's suicide,
then call to mind the dark God of Milton
and the bread that his blindness was fed on:
the long and sweet procedures of his breath,
The rigid satisfaction, death for death.
So godlike and so dark in poetry,
he lies beyond what we can choose to be,
poets cannot choose their own tragedy.

Yet what the poet is, chooses to be,
is the momentum of all poetry,
the momentum of life, the dying breath,
in which life is the transcendence of death,
an unearthly and unnatural bread
and earthly resurrection of the dead.
τοῖς μὲν γὰρ παιδαρίοισιν
ἐστὶ διδάσκαλος ὅστις φράζει,
τοῖσιν δ' ἡβῶσι ποιηταί.
It is schoolmasters who discourse to boys,
but it is poets mature time employs.
A poet is not all that he will be:
his way of changing is his poetry:
his virtues are in nature, and by them
nature's resurrection is his poem.

Or that is what the old poets believed;
the poem and the self that they conceived
begins with the *Symposium* of Plato:
eros is still the most that poets know.
The realist groan and the secular hymn

are lost from eros, and still seeking him.
The river-mists of verse that cling and soak,
the last wild honey dripping down the oak,
the boughs of fresh leaf on the dying tree,
bird tunes of Tennysonian poetry
haunting us, lost in us, as we are lost,
wither in frost. Poetry is that frost.
Because we have said what we had to say
and our beliefs yellow and fall away.
The faith of poets is the last bird-call,
uncouth, neglected, individual.
It is rooted much deeper than the mind
in the language of birds and of mankind
falling like light in the most silent wood.
It is what Mayakovsky understood.
I know the strength of words, I know the beat of words
never applauded from the theatre boxes
but they break coffins loose, they walk away
on their four wooden legs. They let you rot,
they will not print you or publish you,
you lighten girth, gallop, and your hooves ring
down centuries, and iron expresses
creep up to kiss your calloused hands,
poetry. I know the strength of words.
They look like nothing, like a flower dropped
and shattered under the tread of a dancer.
But a man in his soul, in his lips, in his bones . . .

Thinking of my title I am not sure
whether you came expecting a lecture
rather than all these impassioned sayings,
bits of old poems and workshop chippings,
or whether linking the title with Horace
(whose *Ars Poetica* Fraenkel could not face,
it is an intellectual disgrace)
you expected poetry cold in the
aspic of neo-classic theory.
The English poem is a sun that sets.
Observation of poems and poets
reveals death in them and death of belief,
and resurrection in them, the fresh leaf,
that sprouts living out of the dead poem:
poems consume life as the rose his stem.
Philip Larkin's poetry made such sense
that you could rest in complete confidence
whatever he said would be genuine:
and as lively as jazz, as clean as gin.
There are no mysteries, only our lives,
and death, and something in us that deprives
the self of the old self it was wound in:
this is a poem balanced on a pin,
a dazzle of Marvellian mysteries,
a nettle against spring, as our life is.
The trees are coming into leaf
Like something almost being said;

The recent buds relax and spread,
Their greenness is a kind of grief.

Is it that they are born again
And we grow old? No, they die too.
Their yearly trick of looking new
Is written down in rings of grain.

Yet still the unresting castles thresh
In fullgrown thickness every May.
Last year is dead, they seem to say,
Begin afresh, afresh, afresh.

The mysteries of life were in language
when reason shone supreme in its own age,
when faith withered and was disquieted
and only faith in reason was not dead,
in the deep woods there was no smell of smoke,
honey of wild bees dripped in the green oak.
It was in Dryden Hopkins found his wish
for 'naked thew and sinew of English',
and 'my style tends always towards him.'
It is still proper to wander through those dim
mysterious woodlands and clear parklands:
the sea whispers and glitters on those sands.
Since Dryden's age we find less breathing-space,
the lovers are all untrue, and our chase
has nothing now in view. The gods return
to see the crop shaved and the stubble burn

where salt crackled and nightingales complained,
and their lawns were sheep-whitened and moon-stained.
Dryden is most lucid, most reasoning,
most embittered, hungry and life-giving,
each poem is a long philosophy,
a place to walk about, to muse, to be.
From Land a gentle Breeze arose by Night,
Serenely shone the stars, the Moon was bright,
And the Sea trembled with her Silver Light.
. . . Now when the rosie Morn began to rise,
And wav'd her Saffron Streamer thro' the Skies;
When Thetis blush'd in Purple, not her own,
And from her Face the breathing Winds were blown:
A sudden Silence sate upon the Sea,
And sweeping Oars, with Struggling, urge their Way.
The Trojan, from the Main beheld a Wood,
Which thick with Shades, and a brown Horror, stood:
Betwixt the Trees the Tyber took his Course,
With Whirlpools dimpl'd; and with downward Force
That drove the Sand along, he took his Way,
And rowl'd his yellow Billows to the Sea.
About him, and above, and round the Wood,
The Birds that haunt the Borders of his Flood:
That bath'd within, or bask'd upon his side,
To tuneful Songs their narrow Throats apply'd.
The Captain gives Command, the joyful Train
Glide thro' the gloomy Shade, and leave the Main.

How long and slow the movement of it is,
quicker of course than William Morris
and magical without romantic cheat:
with trumpet descant and a thin drum-beat.
How far it is from Homer's poetry,
the banks of flowers and the nodding tree,
personal death, impersonal poetry,
and far from the cold passions of Virgil,
the indignant soul that rushes and is still;
the hero dies and we are left alone,
the dream of Rome is as cold as a stone.
    It was sex that revived the classic age,
sexual passion and ironic rage;
sexual intimacy and sexual dance
are the innocent part of the Renaissance,
which by the way never occurred in Wales,
barely touches the *Canterbury Tales*,
but in English is first heard of in Gower
and in Chaucer's *Troilus* comes to its power.
The early books are tense but in Book Three
love's powerful, pliable intimacy
creates entangled rhythms, fresh language,
a beacon-light to Wyatt and his age:
surf and waves that the sea combs and refines
as Shakespeare in his sonnets combs his lines.
Book by book, Chaucer's *Troilus* changes gear
(the epilogue is an ice-age I fear),
but this is our first recorded affair,

briar roses but with snow in the air,
in verse perfect, in construction unfree,
the first serious English love story:
small wonder poetry arose from it,
and variations of verse and sense and wit,
because our life was still the Atlantic,
intimate passion was still dramatic,
poetry was more than chamber music.
    But poetry seeks out its own extremes,
those drowsy poems that proceed like dreams,
or Marlowe's hollow thunders and fresh rain,
or dying woods and Agamemnon's pain:
or Shakespeare flashing fires in a half-line,
the creamy vein, the yellow celandine.
A poem of one line expires in one,
having done more than most poems have done:
been pungent, modest, memorable, singing,
one with the earth and air, self-echoing,
it is the gravestone set at its own head
to mark the resurrection of the dead.
Though thou the wolf hoar had to priest
though thou him to school set, psalms to learn,
ever be his gears to the grove green.
There are true poems, short, real lines like these
hidden in all natural languages:
poetry in its first natural state
is Homeric, tragic, illiterate,
the shortest and the longest of verses

cluster together where the firelight is,
and what they have in common is one thing,
a long line suitable for chanting:
a line we lost with *Beowulf* and *Gawain*,
a horn–blast we shall never hear again.
Our ears are trained to the Latin iambic,
where we once waved a wand, we beat a stick.
Heroic poetry closer to the sun
takes two lines of our ballads to make one:
In Scarlet town when I was young there was a fair maid
    dwelling.
That all the youths cried lack a day, her name was Barbara
    Allen.
ζάχαρι εἶν' τὸ χέρι του, καὶ τὸ σπαθί του χάρος.
In English the same line is short of breath,
'His hand was sugar, and his sword was death.'
Yet that Latin metre set Shakespeare free,
dramatic verse is our best poetry:
if you reread the sonnets you will find
they are dramatic verses of a kind,
only Shakespeare wrote them or could have done,
of shady poets the best, shadiest one.
Dramatic verse is dead, with all it brings.
The nightingale sings that all the wood rings,
She singeth in her song that the night is too long.
Now our blood has run weak which once ran strong,
we have lost what underlay poetry,
a simple, sensuous intensity

that in the sixties it used to be said
revolution revives, but now that's dead.
What lives will survive in another form,
like the ghost of a calm after the storm.
Smouldering revolutionary wars
drip like blood-dawns from bullet-holes like stars:
the single word Liberty repeated
crows like a cock in the dark over the dead.
    Poetry is a dead horse, it's a mess,
a competition in the weekly press.
Yet Shakespeare's seeds are sleeping in that ground,
fatal and poisonous, and to be found
by who chooses, who searches and who needs,
with resurrection sleeping in his seeds.
We foolish old men have passed our lives long
fiddling with the echoes of a harsh song
in the secure knowledge it will be found:
the bones of Baudelaire lie in that ground.
And as it was surely in Chaucer's day
and in Shakespeare's, so now in our own day
our best hope lies in foreign poetry
and we reroot in foreign poetry.
The old daylight we needed to forget
has withdrawn from our coast: *the violet
has made its home now in the deepening shade,
the final refuge of the exiled soul.*
Poets are exiles: poems are made whole.
In the last century Gautier decreed

writing poems is a gratuitous deed,
useless, non-moral and unnatural
(the view of half our uncles after all),
yet poems cannot be categorized,
they are primitive, they are not civilized,
poems are like a bird's song, natural,
being human they tend to be moral,
they have their use, they linger in the mind,
their spark of eros remains undefined
in all ages, ranks and societies:
eros is more than the mind can quite seize.
Take Jaccottet again, 'Daybreak' again:
You are the light rising on cold rivers
the lark sprung from the field. What simple verse,
and the thought is as primitive as sunrise,
the small skills of poets are mysteries
which like birdsong cannot be fully stated,
the very earth is laid bare and elated.
True poetry never sates, never cloys,
is primitive because it is a noise,
an intricate string of minute noises
expressing what man thinks and feels and is
and civilized society represses.
When the two meet they will conflict headlong
in the most thrilling outburst of pure song,
in Virgil's images, Miltonic verse,
delighted and delightful and perverse.

Pope in his rustic palace makes a stand,
but the world moves, the rope slips in the hand,
holding that verse the civilized hand burns:
poetry must forget all that it learns,
the rhymes, the couplets, the whole bag of tricks:
ancient poetry lies beyond the Styx.
Things come back only when they are unlearnt,
and the hand tingles where it had been burnt,
the noise dies out, the poets rearrange,
it is the noises change and never change.
What lives or dies? The scholar is a drudge,
the hungry poet is the only judge,
yet he longs for the scholar's curious ear:
how Chaucer sounds, what accent had Shakespeare?
When the free bird in the thin bramble sings
his song is learnt by ear: we learn such things,
poet from poet. I could only wish
I saw hope in departments of English.
    Oxford English can offer this defence:
since it was founded its vast influence
has extended through English poetry
and left it on the whole sober and free,
because it has been individual
and curious, with no dogmas at all,
and the canon is always altering:
the result has not been a silent spring.
Elsewhere I warn you these are heady days,
the canon does not alter, it decays.

Old libraries are sold now and not bought,
I hear it said, 'Spenser cannot be taught,
Milton is dodgy' – dodgy was the word,
that is the theatre of the absurd.
What fools abandon lingers in the mind,
it is what I worked all my life to find.
The man who said it moves between great cities
and sits (he said) on twenty-six committees.
Well, we must hop like sparrows for the grain
in the horse-dung, and cycle it again.
The dawn is cold, it takes another tone,
poetry is consumed to the bare bone.
      Ancient Gower brooded in *Pericles*
over a pantomime of mysteries,
Cerimon's resurrection of the dead,
love's long triumph, and God's justice sated.
And years before the Elizabethan stage
Gower's Pygmalion: *the cold image*
he feeleth warm / of flesh and bone and full of life.
Poetry is like Lear on Dover cliff,
all lies, all truth, because wandering Lear
never stood on that edge, never fell there.
And the curse of Timon that brought plague on
Athens was Shakespeare's curse over London.
Let me look back upon thee. O thou wall,
That girdles in those wolves, dive in the earth
And fence not Athens! Matrons, turn incontinent!
Obedience fail in children! Slaves and fools

[22]

Pluck the grave wrinkled Senate from the bench
And minister in their steads! To general filths
Convert i'th'instant, green Virginity -
Do't in your parents' eyes! Bankrupts, hold fast,
Rather than render back, out with your knives
And cut your trusters' throats! Bound servants, steal!
Large-handed robbers your grave masters are,
And pill by law! Maid, to thy master's bed,
Thy mistress is o'th'brothel. Son of sixteen,
Pluck the lined crutch from thy old limping sire,
With it beat out his brains! Piety and fear,
Religion to the gods, peace, justice, truth,
Domestic awe, night-rest and neighbourhood,
Instruction, manners, mysteries, and trades,
Degrees, observances, customs and laws,
Decline to your confounding contraries,
Confusion live! – Plagues incident to men,
Your potent and infectious fevers heap
On Athens, ripe for stroke! Thou cold sciatica,
Cripple our senators, that their limbs may halt
As lamely as their manners. Lust and liberty
Creep in the minds and marrows of our youth,
That 'gainst the stream of virtue they may strive
And drown themselves in riot. Itches, blains
Sow all the Athenian bosoms, and their crop
Be general leprosy! Breath infect breath,
That their society as their friendship may
Be merely poison! . . . Timon will to the woods.

Has this curse not a very modern sound?
The seeds of Shakespeare's curse sleep in our ground.
But poetry remains itself alone,
fresh as snow, cold as water, hard as stone;
and only poetry can colonize
the island or the untrodden paradise;
language roots in the mouth of the first dead
under the new crops in their shallow bed,
the illiterate and the anonymous,
feeds on provincial words and the green forest:
rising or dipping sun mean east and west.
Homer had no word for the north or south,
ice in the mouth or desert in the mouth,
yet for the wind he had a hundred names.
Poetry is still playing the same games,
ten thousand generations from Adam,
and the core of the poem is *I am*.
Of all definitions of poetry
what it is or has been or can be
I think Pasternak's is the most sublime:
'eternity's hostage in the hands of time.'
Aristotle the old philosopher
says the end of philosophy is wonder,
and eternity's hostage is wonderful,
time's hand shapes it, we watch the poem cool
till we can handle it, expatriates
of that wonder which poetry creates.
Plato glibly overshadows us: we

have trouble with the word eternity,
we are not citizens of wonderland.
I know only what I hold in my hand,
poetry is godlike, not absolute good,
if God did not exist, poetry would.
What is caught in the margins of language
trapped in chance words like a bird in a cage,
has no status in being or logic:
poetry is a kind of cheap magic:
but poems have a right to speak and be,
and I love them and their cheap mystery.
They comfort me with their familiar chime,
eternity's hostage in the hand of time.

    We may be the last Europeans you see
to take eternity so seriously.
Time is really a new idea of ours,
hence the English obsession with clock-towers
(Russian eternity consumes all hours).
Only inside a poem can time play
and still be perfect, die and live and stay,
and there time is eternal in a way.
A timelessness hangs around verse-endings
and within poems time may fold his wings.
Waller's best poem holds time in its hands,
being *Battle of the Summer Islands,*
fought between the islanders and two whales.
He longs to be there and away he sails
over the always blue, spice-breathing seas

and like a native settles down: *palm trees*
Under the shadow of whose friendly boughs
They sit, carousing where their liquor grows.
. . . Such is the mould, that the bless'd tenant feeds
On precious fruits, and pays his rent in weeds.
With candied plantains, and the juicy pine,
On choicest melons, and sweet grapes, they dine,
And with potatoes fat their wanton swine.
There is eternity in timeless time,
locked in an old verse, summoned in a rhyme,
drifting to life again out of its dust,
and all the halleluiahs of the just
will not disturb that black man from his tree,
ruffle the surface of the baroque sea
or make time run back from reality.

    Poems are real and poems are impure,
in their beginning as in their closure,
heaven is what poems cannot endure.
Paradise is a bag of monkey-tricks,
a vision of Italian politics,
and love is not pure love if it can rhyme,
it is a hostage in the hands of time.
The human heart, that impure origin,
alone determines what is genuine,
and can discern it in tones of the voice:
the slurred rhythm, the small, particular noise
of music's innocent complexities,
bright eyes, pink cheeks, transparent mysteries.

Eternity sings in a bed of sands
when Cotton's *floods do clap their liquid hands*.
Eternity applauded the baroque,
poetry shook with the delightful shock,
when heavy fancies of the court and stage
cut crisp in words brought in a golden age.
Gold never tarnishes but melts away,
it is most prodigal with dying day:
the old colour of honey and the sun
that names a golden age cannot make one,
darkness and green remained our mysteries,
there was no honey dripping down the trees.
    Poetry is vision and is truth,
grass crown of age, maturity of youth:
because the imagination is truthful
and Blake truthfully wrote that heaven is full
of angels in their thousands at sunrise.
If grace grant thee to go in this wise,
Thou shalt see in thyself Truth sit in thy heart,
In a chain of charity, as thou a child were.
. . . *The light followed the Lord into the low earth.*
Poetry is to this degree faith
that it cannot be abolished by death,
the limits of its language are more clear
than the stars are, but also mistier.
A wise man wrestles where a child will know
how the world goes or things in poems go.
Thou shalt see in thyself Truth sit in thy heart

by William Langland's art and by Blake's art:
the vision is the visionary's part
by whose pleased spirit and at whose hand we
take some of our beliefs from poetry,
from Christian or pagan equally,
poetry being natural to man,
and the soul being by nature pagan.
So in the death of Christ as in his birth,
light followed the Lord into the low earth.
        Of all arts and in all its mystery
poetry is the most deeply earthly.
Do you believe that grieving of the mind
left Tennyson purified or refined
in his long fit of deathly thoughts, or worse,
unequalled majesty of personal verse?
Many thoughts flocked round him when Hallam died,
In Memoriam is unrarefied,
it is individual, true poetry
with textures that we feel and smell and see.
And yet this is poetry of spirit
with a full-grown Victorian soul in it,
stoical and luxuriant and ill-starred
as an angel of stone in a churchyard.
Calm is the morn without a sound,
        Calm as to suit a calmer grief,
        And only through the faded leaf
The chestnut pattering to the ground:

Calm and deep peace on this high wold,
    And on these dews that drench the furze
    And all the silvery gossamers
That twinkle into green and gold:

Calm and still light on yon great plain
    That sweeps with all its autumn bowers,
    And crowded farms and lessening towers,
To mingle with the bounding main:

Calm and deep peace in this wide air
    These leaves that redden to the fall:
    And in my heart, if calm at all,
If any calm, a calm despair:

Calm on the seas, and silver sleep,
    And waves that sway themselves in rest,
    And dead calm in that noble breast
Which heaves but with the heaving deep.
One kind of grief was never better stated,
one landscape never better celebrated:
no world so hung round one departed friend,
no sentence so mused to its deadly end,
deadly and physical and dramatic,
motionless end of motion: all one trick:
a trick of the heart though, as of the poem.
Notebooks fill up but poems empty them,
the poet shivered backwards to belief

and in one poem emptied years of grief,
years of controlled thought, of uncontrolled sense,
of landscape and the downs and their silence.
　　The greatest poets of our century
in English make us deeply uneasy,
because for better and also for worse
they wrote their own lives raw into their verse:
Pound died as mad as dying Hercules,
Yeats in desire and rage, and both of these
half in love with political violence,
folly of proud minds, madness of proud sense.
Tom Eliot, among these three greatest,
declined into his gentlemanly west,
then woke one day in love, married, and then
scarcely wrote anything ever again.
I have the greatest sympathy with him,
I even love his late verse and the dim
and Christian capers he wrote for the stage,
verse theatre is a therapy for old age:
if it could be more he'd have made it so.
The hardest thing for poets is to let go:
the rope still burns and the hand is still burnt.
From Pound you can still learn as I have learnt
the ABC of the whole modern movement,
forget how he arrived or where he went,
he was a poet by the hardest test:
Eliot's letters to and from Pound are best.
I have feared William Yeats as Larkin did,

those hollow thunders and those raw cries hid
more madness than he knew, more that was false,
thrills by hindsight at the Waterloo waltz,
all the exaggerations of Byron
without the honesty, face painted on
(almost) for a senate of assassins,
bumpkins and sly fellows, a phoney prince.
    And yet Yeats is a great, great poet
whom I admit I never can forget.
Still, he is wit's and scarcely nature's child
and about as honest as Oscar Wilde:
but that he lived into his serious age
and that his verses burn the dusty stage.
Of these three poets it was only he
who touched the last limits of poetry,
as that had been physically defined
in his time by the ear and voice and mind.
Stress metres ended and down Kipling went,
but Yeats was saved by his Irish accent.
It was the language altered: one forgets
such a change is first noticed by poets.
    As for the modern, that began in France,
and to its music we have danced our dance.
By one of history's spectacular twists,
two at least of the greatest modernists
were anti-modernist founding fathers
by the majestic sweep of their great verse:
New England Lowell, Russian Pasternak

had heard the river heave and the ice crack
and lived to see all nature musical
as it had been, yet transformed after all,
because language first transforms in the ear,
then the poem descants on what we hear.
But there is also personal progress:
the condition of success is unsuccess,
and the change of a language in a life-span
may be less than the changes in a man.
Lowell's *Notebook* of 1970
and *History* of 1973
differ by vigorous muscular strength
exercised in poems of the same length,
the unrhymed sonnet or the quatorzaine;
it was his vice to do things over again.
It was his vice, maybe it was his craze
just as Picasso's was in his last days,
endless, prodigal creativity:
but I feel the loose muscle in *History*.
Notebook was one long poem he did say,
and the revision like cutting away
the marble from the figure in the rock.
What I liked was the metronomic clock
controlling history as the dead soul
in the live poems swayed their barcarole,
their dying notes, their individual tone,
their seagulls' cries ripped open to the bone.

And poetry is as history is,
the consequences sleep in their causes,
the world to come hangs on a poet's rhyme
but we are not aesthetes of future time,
Blake's head is nothing but a dreaming bone,
his angel lay sleeping in a stone;
something in him quarried to set it free:
cutting away that rock is poetry,
the truth of poetry is history.
　　And all the old aesthetes wasted their days
refining down the world into a phrase,
in love with ghosts of roses, scents of doubt,
finding the world too coarse to write about:
Narcissus drowned in one long wavering note,
nothing to say, no birdsong in his throat.
Yet there arises one compelling ghost,
one trumpet voice, the art's father almost,
the aesthete Yeats, a voice that carries still
when the horsemen have vanished from the hill.
. . . *At Mooneen he had leaped a place*
So perilous that half the astonished meet
Had shut their eyes; and where was it
He rode a race without a bit?
And yet his mind outran the horses' feet.

We dreamed that a great painter had been born
To cold Clare rock and Galway rock and thorn,
To that stern colour and that delicate line

That are our secret discipline
Wherein the gazing heart doubles her might.
The poem goes off there, as poetry,
it is not tied down to reality.
The only painter I know Irish-born
is Francis Bacon, hates hunting, and is torn
by deeper stresses than that idiot zoo
of national bogies Yeats admitted to.

 It is something to cut deep, to cut new,
we need unlikely medicines, pursue
the truth and true passion and true courage.
The pleasant verse of a complacent age
is claustrophobic and means death to us:
Sir John Denham's best poem is 'To Morpheus'.
The poetry of the possession of heaven
is merely charming to unburied men.
We are not in that chorus which was picked
to chant with Francis or with Benedict,
we mope in ruined cloisters, and our Christ
is what Ulysses looked for in the west:
the gilded waves and the sea-monster's hum,
the islands of the blest, the Christ to come.
He did not lead the Russian revolution;
he does not guard the British constitution.
Tennyson's patriotism is stinking air,
Blake was half mad, and Blok died in despair.
The truth of poetry is a dying breath.
Pasternak says the fresh air smelt of death

in our days, and to open a window
was to open a vein.
                    It has been so,
and now of our tormented century
what will live longer than his poetry?
We all live, we are immortal spirit,
we nest in our poem, we live in it,
yet when poets die and their work is done
the greatest poem is the unwritten one.
In our fresh May, in our leafless November,
it is the unanswered question we remember,
the unwritten poem is the eternal muse,
poems like fallen leaves drift and confuse
and we lie down in languorous sunsets:
the sun falls out of heaven and forgets
all the music of poetry and its pains,
only the unwritten poem remains,
thrilling in Andrew Marvell, close in Donne,
unattained, always nearly the next one.
If the poet turns from it, it comes near,
soars in seasons, lives in the dying year,
speaking in ragged birds' voices maybe
or nightingales of the last century.
The poet's truth is what the poet can,
there is no expression of the whole man.
In his bones lives a wind-torn loud something:
Destroyer and creator, Shelley said,
the spirit of a wind raising the dead.

Only the herdsman crying to the herds
demystifying unpretentious words
which are somehow immediate to the heart
utters mere life, which is the poet's art.
A child can exercise it, shepherds can,
or some illiterate imprisoned man;
we sift through old poems as gardeners
gather dead leaves that the wind hardly stirs.
This is our service, because immortal
spirit is trees that live by leaves that fall.
We are religious at life's funeral.

    I fear the time when this will not be so,
when poetry's occasions seem to grow
into one complex intellectual act,
but the occasions of spirit contract
into the carving of a cherry-stone,
and poetry dies back into the bone:
when poetry belongs to colleges,
a subject only for remarks like these,
and one by one the great examples go,
too difficult to read, too hard to know,
when poems illustrate old politics
and new critics and all such monkey-tricks,
books crumble and the reprints cost too much
being made just for colleges and such.

    Poets like Gower are doomed I assume
(he's out of print, Bodley's lost a volume).
Once the transmission of the poet's art

was in the ear, through poems learnt by heart.
That skill is running out into the sand.
Against this withering I take my stand.
Look back at Matthew Arnold whose complaint
was against all things marginal and quaint,
and yet he loved the Afghans and the Irish,
complained there were not critics in English
like the critical community in France.
How happy those days seem from a distance.
Leavis laboured for the truly central,
Eliot's centre was not there at all.
What is central? The individual
as Larkin saw: art, whose *rough-tongued bell* . . .
Insists I too am individual.
The one centre of English poetry
and the one centre there can ever be
is the individual, obstinate soul:
poetry is poems, never the whole
nation, the whole tradition, the whole man,
but snail-sensitive, antiquarian,
bathed in fire, making things, breaking them,
spirit, dry bones, blind eyes of the poem.
Rumi said, *You see through each cloak I wear*
Know if I speak without mouth or language.
The world is drunk on its desire for words:
I am the slave of the Master of silence.
There is a silence beyond poetry,
and poetry reaches to that silence

or poetry punctuates a silence,
or it is punctuated with silence.
Poetry is the silence between lines,
it is a gesture of quite silent signs.
It is wingbeats, the white swan's dissolution,
unknown to schools of earthly elocution:
the imprisoned spirit echoing on bone,
the flight of the alone from the alone.
When that withers, poetry is undone:
the world hovers round it with kind advice,
but poetry's as lost as paradise.

NOTES AND REFERENCES

Page 10: John Milton, *Paradise Lost* Book III, 41–44.

Page 11: Ibid. III, 212.

Aristophanes, *Frogs* 1054–5.

Page 12: Vladimir Mayakovsky, last section of his final poem.

Pages 13–14: Philip Larkin, 'The Trees'. From *High Windows* (1974), quoted by kind permission of Faber & Faber Ltd.

Page 15: John Dryden's Virgil: *Aeneid* Book VII, 9 ff.

Page 17: *Oxford Book of Medieval English Verse*, no. 278. 'Gears' means instinct and habit and inclination.

Page 18: 'Barbara Allen', anonymous English ballad.

Erotokritos of Kornaros, Book I.

Oxford Book of Medieval English Verse, no. 333.

Page 19: Bei Dao, 'Declaration'. See his *The August Sleepwalker*, Anvil, 1989.

Philippe Jaccottet, 'Au petit jour'. From *Ignorance* (1957), quoted by kind permission of Gallimard. See the bilingual *Selected Poems* translated by Derek Mahon, Penguin, 1988.

Page 20: Philippe Jaccottet, ibid.

Page 22: John Gower, *Confessio Amantis* IV, 422–3. Cf. Christopher Ricks, *The Force of Poetry* pp. 27–29.

Pages 22–23: Shakespeare, *Timon of Athens* Act IV Scene 1.

Page 24: 'eternity's hostage...': from Boris Pasternak's poem 'When the Weather Clears'.

Page 26: Edmund Waller, as on page 25.

Page 27: Charles Cotton, 'Christmas Day, 1659'.

William Langland, *Piers Plowman* 5, 615.

Page 28: Ibid. 18, 239.

Pages 28–29: Alfred Tennyson, *In Memoriam* XI.

Pages 33–34: W.B. Yeats, 'In Memory of Major Robert Gregory'.

Page 37: Philip Larkin, 'Reasons for Attendance'. From *The Less Deceived* (1955), quoted by kind permission of The Marvell Press.

Andrew Harvey, from *Love's Fire – recreations of Rumi* (1988), quoted by kind permission of Jonathan Cape Ltd.